W9-BQE-699

Andrew McCutchen

By Jon M. Fishman

AMAZING
ATHLETES

Lerner Publications • Minneapolis

Copyright © 2015 by Lerner Publishing Group, Inc.

Lerner Publications Company
A division of Lerner Publishing Group, Inc.
241 First Avenue North
Minneapolis, MN 55401 USA

For reading levels and more information, look up this title at www.lernerbooks.com.

The Cataloging-in-Publication Data for *Andrew McCutchen* is on file at the Library of Congress.
ISBN: 978-1-4677-8157-2 (lib. bdg. : alk. paper)
ISBN: 978-1-4677-8158-9 (pbk.)
ISBN: 978-1-4677-8159-6 (EB pdf)

Manufactured in the United States of America
1 – BP – 12/31/14

TABLE OF CONTENTS

Andrew McCutchen steps up to bat against the Philadelphia Phillies.

PIRATE CAPTAIN

Pittsburgh Pirates **center fielder** Andrew McCutchen strolled toward home plate. He stepped into the **batter's box**. He tapped the plate with his bat and raised it above his right shoulder. Andrew was ready for the pitch.

Andrew and the Pirates were playing against the Philadelphia Phillies on September 10, 2014. The game was held at Citizens Bank Park in Philadelphia. The Pirates were in second place in their **division** behind the St. Louis Cardinals. With only a few weeks left in the season, every game was important.

The Pirates have won the World Series five times: 1909, 1925, 1960, 1971, and 1979.

Fans watch Andrew in action at Citizens Bank Park.

The pitcher threw the baseball. Andrew leaned back and raised his left leg. He took a mighty swing. Crack! The ball streaked to the outfield. It sailed over the head of the Philadelphia center fielder and bounced off the outfield wall.

Andrew sends the ball flying in the fifth inning of the game.

Andrew races toward home plate.

Andrew raced around the bases as the ball rolled on the ground. He is one of Major League Baseball's (MLB) fastest runners. He was almost to third base by the time a Phillies player picked up the ball. Andrew didn't slow down. He cruised around third base and headed for home.

When he crossed home plate, Andrew was running so fast that his helmet fell off. It was an **inside-the-park home run**! Pittsburgh won the game, 6–3.

Andrew says that part of his success comes from knowing what to expect in the batter's box. "It's having a game plan and knowing what the pitcher is going to do," he said. "I'm getting wiser." A wiser Andrew is a scary thought for opposing pitchers. His wisdom on the field has already helped earn him the 2013 Most Valuable Player (MVP) Award in the National League (NL). After Andrew received the award, Pittsburgh **manager** Clint Hurdle summed up his star player in a few words. "[Andrew] has a hunger to hit," Hurdle said.

Andrew loses his helmet as he crosses home plate.

Andrew was born in Fort Meade, Florida. The area is a popular place for canoeing and kayaking.

YOUNG FAMILY

In 1986, Petrina Swan was a junior at Fort Meade High School (FMHS) in Fort Meade, Florida. Her boyfriend, Lorenzo McCutchen, was a sophomore at the school. That spring the young couple told their families that Petrina was pregnant. Andrew Stefan McCutchen was born in Fort Meade on October 10, 1986.

Andrew gets a hug from his mom, Petrina.

As high school students, Petrina and Lorenzo found it difficult to support a baby. Lorenzo and Petrina decided to split up. "We knew we loved each other, but that wasn't enough, even though we had a baby," Petrina said.

Andrew lived with his mother, grandmother, aunt, and cousins while his parents finished school. Lorenzo played on FMHS's baseball, football, and basketball teams. He worked at a grocery store in his spare time. After graduating from high school, Petrina started going to Polk State College in Winter Haven, Florida. She played on the school's volleyball team.

In 1988, Lorenzo accepted a **scholarship** to play football at Carson-Newman College in Jefferson City, Tennessee. Most nights, he spoke with Andrew on the phone. But Lorenzo couldn't stand to be away from his son for long. He soon returned to Fort Meade.

Fort Meade is in central Florida, east of Tampa.

When Andrew was five years old, Lorenzo and Petrina got married. The family moved to nearby Bartow. The town was closer to Lorenzo's job working in a mine. Bartow also had a public school called Union Academy (UA).

Andrew's parents wanted him to attend UA someday. They knew it was a good school that expected students to work hard at their studies. After elementary school, Andrew started going to UA.

Andrew and his dad spent many hours together practicing baseball. Lorenzo wanted Andrew to think of home plate as his house. "I used to tell him to swing hard and protect his house," Lorenzo said. The practice paid off. By the age of 11, Andrew was the best player on his Dixie Youth Baseball team.

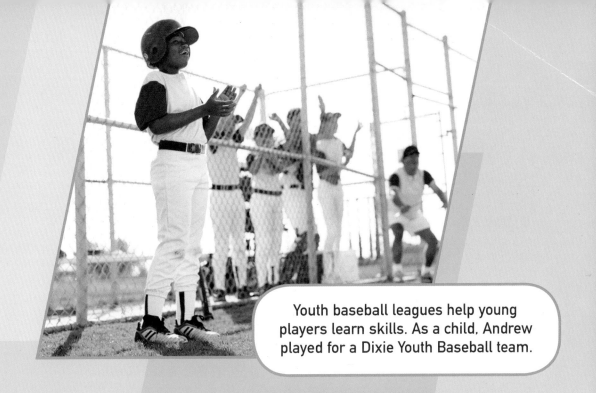

Youth baseball leagues help young players learn skills. As a child, Andrew played for a Dixie Youth Baseball team.

HIGH SCHOOL STAR

In 2000, Jeff Tofanelli was the manager of FMHS's **varsity** baseball team. He saw Andrew playing for his Dixie Youth Baseball team. Tofanelli could tell right away that Andrew was a special ballplayer. The coach was impressed with the way Andrew swung the bat. Tofanelli asked Andrew and his family to switch schools.

He wanted Andrew to play baseball at FMHS. The school included grades 7–12. Andrew could finish middle school there. The McCutchens agreed to the move. Andrew became the only eighth-grade player on FMHS's varsity baseball team.

As a 13-year-old on the varsity team, Andrew was in for a big challenge. He was younger than all of his teammates. Some of the players were 18-year-old men. Coach Tofanelli wasn't sure how Andrew would handle the situation.

As a child, Andrew loved baseball. He admired baseball players such as Ken Griffey Jr. *(left)*.

"There's a big difference physically among boys at those ages," Tofanelli said.

Andrew's nickname is Cutch.

Andrew proved that he was ready for the varsity team. He played **shortstop**. Shortstop is one of the most difficult fielding positions in baseball. But Andrew's quick feet and strong throwing arm helped him keep up with the older players. He was even more impressive in the batter's box. His .591 **batting average** was the best on the team. It was the highest varsity baseball batting average in the county.

In eighth grade, Andrew also played on FMHS's **junior varsity** football team. In one game, he scored five touchdowns. That was his last game with the team. The coaches moved him up to the varsity team.

The next year, Andrew continued to star on the varsity baseball team. A Major League Baseball (MLB) **scout** watched Andrew play that season. He thought the young player's blazing speed could be put to better use in the outfield. Tofanelli agreed. Before the start of the next season, he moved Andrew to center field. As a sophomore, Andrew also showed off his fast footwork in track and field. He helped FMHS win the state championship in the 4x100-meter **relay**.

Baseball scouts such as these attend high school games to look for future MLB players.

Andrew fields the ball before a game in 2004.

GETTING NOTICED

Andrew spent a lot of time exercising and playing sports. But he still got good grades in school. He also stayed out of trouble. His parents expected no less of him. Lorenzo and Petrina wanted their son to always behave in a respectful manner and honor their values.

After Andrew started driving, Lorenzo found a CD in his son's truck that contained bad language. "You know we don't listen to this type of music," Lorenzo said. Then he broke the CD in half.

In 2004, Andrew began his senior season at FMHS. His batting average for the year was over .700. He hit with power and played stellar defense in the outfield. He also kept up his good grades.

Andrew's outstanding work, both in the classroom and on the baseball field, earned him a lot of attention. The University of Florida (UF) offered Andrew a baseball scholarship. Then, in June 2005, MLB held its annual **draft**. The Pittsburgh Pirates had the 11th pick. The team didn't know which player to choose.

Andrew likes to draw and write poetry.

The University of Florida campus is in Gainesville, Florida.

Pittsburgh scout Rob Sidwell had been watching Andrew play for years. Sidwell loved what he saw of Andrew on the baseball field. The scout also liked Lorenzo and Petrina and the values they'd passed on to their son. "I was so impressed with his family," Sidwell said. "Especially with a high school kid, the family background is so important."

Andrew waits for a pitch during a game on July 29, 2005.

Sidwell convinced the Pirates to choose Andrew with the 11th pick in the draft. The young outfielder was thrilled. He turned down the scholarship offer from UF. Instead, he was about to become a professional baseball player.

The Pirates wanted Andrew to gain experience in the **minor leagues**. He began the 2005 season playing for the Gulf Coast League Pirates in Bradenton, Florida. Over the next few seasons, Andrew played for minor-league teams in Pennsylvania, North Carolina, and Indiana. In 2009, he was finally called up to Pittsburgh to play for the Pirates.

Andrew played for the Hickory Crawdads in 2006. The team plays in Hickory, North Carolina.

Andrew showed impressive skills in his first major-league game.

MOST VALUABLE PIRATE

On June 4, 2009, Andrew played his first MLB game. He tried to relax and have fun playing the sport he loved. "I know if I do that, I'll have success," Andrew said. In his first at bat, he pounded the ball to the outfield for a base hit. He had two hits and scored three runs in the game. Pittsburgh beat the New York Mets, 11–6.

On August 1, 2009, Lorenzo and Petrina traveled to Pittsburgh to watch the Pirates play. It was their first chance to attend a game since Andrew had joined the team. The day was also special for another reason. It was the couple's 17th wedding anniversary. Andrew put on a show for his parents. He blasted three home runs to help the Pirates beat the Washington Nationals, 11–6. "He gave us an awesome anniversary present," Lorenzo said.

Petrina has sung the National Anthem before the start of two Pirates games.

Petrina sings the National Anthem at the start of a Pirates game on October 1, 2013.

Andrew waves to the crowd after hitting a home run against the Washington Nationals on August 1, 2009.

Andrew hit .286 with 12 home runs during his **rookie** season. He continued to play well in 2010 and 2011. The Pirates rewarded Andrew with a huge **contract**. The team agreed to pay him $51.5 million over the next six years.

In 2012, Andrew's batting average of .327 was the third best in MLB. He also crushed 31 home runs and ran for 20 **stolen bases**. He finished third in NL MVP voting.

Andrew steals a base in August 2012.

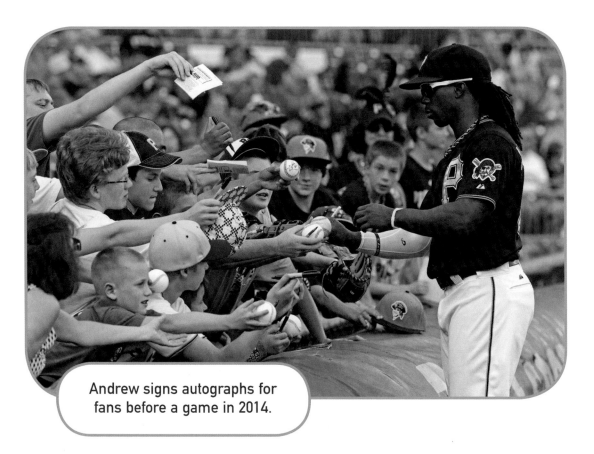

Andrew signs autographs for fans before a game in 2014.

Andrew began using his fame and fortune to help people in need. He and the Pirates started Cutch's Crew. The group gives money and time to help youth baseball teams in big cities. Andrew also gives his time to support the Children's Hospital of Pittsburgh and other groups.

The 2013 season was one of Andrew's best. He hit .317 with 21 home runs and 27 stolen bases. He was named NL MVP. After the season, Andrew and his girlfriend, Maria Hanslovan, appeared on *The Ellen DeGeneres Show*. With cameras rolling, Andrew got down on one knee and asked Maria to marry him. She said yes!

Andrew and his girlfriend, Maria, pose on the red carpet at the American Music Awards on November 24, 2013.

Andrew slides to catch a fly ball in the outfield.

Andrew is one of MLB's biggest superstars. In 2014, he was voted to the All-Star Game for the fourth time. Even better, he has helped make the Pirates a winning team. With Andrew in the outfield, Pittsburgh's future is bright.

Selected Career Highlights

2014 Named to the MLB All-Star Game for the fourth time

2013 Named to the MLB All-Star Game for the third time
Hit .317 with 21 home runs and 27 stolen bases
Won the NL MVP Award

2012 Named to the MLB All-Star Game for the second time
Hit .327 with 31 home runs and 20 stolen bases
Finished third in MVP voting

2011 Named to the MLB All-Star Game for the first time
Hit .259 with 23 home runs and 23 stolen bases

2010 Hit .286 with 16 home runs and 33 stolen bases

2009 Hit .286 with 12 home runs and 22 stolen bases
Called up to play 108 games with the Pittsburgh Pirates
Played in 20 games for the Indianapolis Indians

2008 Played in 135 games for the Indianapolis Indians

2007 Played in 118 games for the Altoona Curve
Played in 17 games for the Indianapolis Indians

2006 Played in 114 games for the Hickory Crawdads
Played in 20 games for the Altoona Curve

2005 Played in 13 games for the Williamsport Crosscutters
Played in 45 games for the Gulf Coast League Pirates
Chosen by the Pittsburgh Pirates with the 11th overall pick in the MLB draft

2004 Played baseball, football, and ran track at FMHS

2003 Played baseball, football, and ran track at FMHS
Helped the FMHS track team win the state championship in the 4x100-meter relay

2002 Played baseball, football, and ran track at FMHS

2001 Played baseball, football, and ran track at FMHS

2000 Became a member of the FMHS varsity baseball team
Scored five touchdowns in one game on the FMHS junior varsity football team

Glossary

batter's box: the areas on both sides of home plate where the batter can stand

batting average: a number that describes how often a baseball player gets a hit

center fielder: a person who plays in the middle of the outfield

contract: an agreement signed by a player and a team that states the amount of money the player is paid and the number of years he will play

division: a group of teams that compete for first place in their group and play more often against one another. MLB has six divisions.

draft: a yearly event in which professional teams take turns choosing new players from a selected group

inside-the-park home run: when a player gets a hit that does not leave the playing field but still allows him to run all the way around the bases to score

junior varsity: a school sports team that is usually for younger players

manager: the head coach of a baseball team

minor leagues: groups of teams where players improve their skills and prepare to advance to MLB

relay: a race between teams in which different athletes run different parts of the race

rookie: a first-year player

scholarship: money given to students by schools or other groups to help pay for school

scout: a person who judges the abilities of athletes

shortstop: a baseball player who takes the position on the field between second base and third base

stolen bases: when base runners move from one base to the next without the batter getting a hit. A runner often steals a base while the pitcher is throwing the ball to home plate.

varsity: the top sports team at a school

Further Reading & Websites

Doeden, Matt. *The World Series: Baseball's Biggest Stage*. Minneapolis: Millbrook Press, 2014.

Fishman, Jon M. *Clayton Kershaw*. Minneapolis: Lerner Publications, 2015.

Kennedy, Mike, and Mark Stewart. *Long Ball: The Legend and Lore of the Home Run*. Minneapolis: Millbrook Press, 2006.

Major League Baseball: The Official Site
http://mlb.mlb.com/home
The official Major League Baseball website provides fans with game results, statistics, schedules, and biographies of players.

The Official Site of the Pittsburgh Pirates
http://pittsburgh.pirates.mlb.com/index.jsp?c_id=pit
The official website of the Pittsburgh Pirates includes the team schedule and game results, biographies of Andrew McCutchen and other players and coaches, and much more.

Sports Illustrated Kids
http://www.sikids.com
The *Sports Illustrated Kids* website covers all sports, including baseball.

LERNER

SOURCE

Expand learning beyond the printed book. Download free, complementary educational resources for this book from our website, www.lerneresource.com.

Index

Photo Acknowledgments

The images in this book are used with the permission of: © Rich Schultz/Getty Images, p. 4; AP Photo/Matt Slocum, p. 5; © Bill Streicher/USA TODAY Sports, p. 6; Derik Hamilton/Icon Sportswire CGY/Newscom, pp. 7, 8; © Zuma Press/Alamy, p. 9; © Justin K. Aller/Getty Images, p. 10; © Ken Chernus/The Image Bank/Getty Images, p. 13; © Jonathan Daniel/Allsport/Getty Images, p. 14; © V.J. Lovero/Sports Illustrated/Getty Images, p. 16; © Diamond Images/Getty Images, p. 17; © Jeff Greenberg/Alamy, p. 19; © Joy R. Absalon/USA TODAY Sports, p. 20; AP Photo/Tom Priddy/Four Seam Images, p. 21; © Jerry Lai/USA TODAY Sports, p. 22; © Joe Sargent/MLB Photos via Getty Images, p. 23; AP Photo/ Gene J. Puskar, pp. 24, 26; © Rob Leiter/MLB Photos via Getty Images, p. 25; © Press Line Photos/Splash News/CORBIS, p. 27; © Otto Greule Jr./Getty Images, p. 28; © Justin Edmonds/Getty Images, p. 29.

Front cover: © Dennis Poroy/Getty Images.

Main body text set in Caecilia LT Std 55 Roman 16/28.
Typeface provided by Adobe Systems.